365 Random Thoughts

In the style of Wittgenstein, Lichtenberg & Carlin

Stephen Doty

365 RANDOM THOUGHTS
IN THE STYLE OF WITTGENSTEIN,
LICHTENBERG & CARLIN

iUniverse books may be ordered through booksellers or by contacting:

iUniverse
1663 Liberty Drive
Bloomington, IN 47403
www.iuniverse.com
844-349-9409

ISBN: 978-1-4401-7416-2 (sc)
ISBN: 978-1-4401-7417-9 (e)

Print information available on the last page.

iUniverse rev. date: 12/06/2023

What we do is to bring words back from their metaphysical to their everyday use.

What we are destroying is nothing but houses of cards and we are clearing up the ground of language on which they stand.

I believe it might interest a philosopher, one who can think himself, to read my notes. For even if I have hit the mark only rarely, he would recognize what targets I had been ceaselessly aiming at.

The question "How do I know..." drags out the language-game, or else does away with it.

–Ludwig Wittgenstein

Once we know our weaknesses they cease to do us any harm.

A punishment in a dream is still a punishment. On the utility of dreams.

Confidence in one's strength is strength.

–Georg Lichtenberg

The decay and disintegration of this culture is astonishingly amusing if you are emotionally detached from it.

I'm sixty years of age. That's 16 Celsius.

–George Carlin

Introduction

I kept a notebook in my briefcase from 1996-2009 and wrote down brief remarks when I felt the urge, typically while drinking tea at Starbucks in Florida and at Jaho in Massachusetts. I've looked through those notebooks recently and picked out entries that I believe others will enjoy. As a reader, I appreciate aphoristic refinement and strive for that as a writer. Although my tone may be pedagogical at times, this remains more my study than my teaching. The first twelve chapters have thirty remarks each, and the last one has five.

I want to thank Prof. Frank Wilson, who taught philosophy at Bucknell University for over twenty years, for reviewing a draft copy of this book and for making some suggestions for its improvement.

The image on the front cover alludes to a remark on page three concerning probabilities. Cover design by Team Kafka at the publishing house.

"Hey, that's a good cabernet -- let it breathe!"

1

When you buy stock in a company that makes diapers, it's hard to time the bottom.

Aging gracefully is difficult. I've gone from riding scooters with a Duchess to visiting Hooters on crutches.

Politicians buy votes by promising to spend government money. That's why the USA must eventually go broke, like California – because good politics is bad economics, and good economics is bad politics.

Why don't I believe in astrology? –Because I'm a Taurus. We're skeptical.

A travel tip. If you ever find yourself among a tribe of cannibals and learn that they also practice circumcision, do not eat the onion rings.

Beaches keep banning thongs – with no bottom in sight.

For a romantic movie to work for women, they have to like the idea of sex with the leading man; to work for men, vice versa. "Titanic" worked for women but not so much for men. Kate Winslet was no Raquel Welch or Sophia Loren. And if she gained any more weight, James Cameron would have reshot the movie with Kathy Bates as Rose Dawson and released it as "Thigh-tanic."

When a health insurance company refuses to pay for a colostomy, who's left holding the *bag?*

After Lady Diana died, I invented a tacky drink called the "Paparazzi." *A shot of Crown Royal with a chaser.*

If you put two identical cigarette lighters side-by-side, you get a perfect match.

How many members of the National Organization for Women does it take to change a light bulb? –Four. One to change it, and three to chant, "See! We don't need a man!"

Most people are too frugal for their own good and don't realize it. They overspend in one or two areas only. A woman with sixty pairs of high-heels will not buy a new fry pan or hairbrush, despite needing them, because she wants to feel thrifty. A man with forty watches will not spring for new socks and cutlery, so he can feel frugal. Posh Spice has spent two million dollars on a hundred designer handbags. I wonder what she scrimps on around the house to compensate for that – bathmats?

Funny how people don't change. I knew a kid in school who was always getting into trouble, always pushing the envelope. Today, he's a mailman.

What makes the lottery, or any casino game, a sucker's bet is not the slim chance of winning but the relatively small payoff when you win. The issue is not *frequency* but *expected value*. At a craps table, rolling double sixes pays thirty times your wager. Betting a hundred dollars would be smart if it paid thirty-eight times, since the odds are 35:1 against it. Losing the vast majority of dice throws is irrelevant.

My grandfather started with nothing and worked his way up to utter destitution.

Yes, I've seen poverty, and I've seen it up close. In fact, my parents once asked the limo driver to pull over and stop, so I could get a good look.

After watching one episode of "The Sopranos," I got the *tenor* of the show.

In order to drop clichés like a bad habit, a writer must pull himself up by his own bootstraps, go that extra mile, and then draw a line in the sand. Oops.

Here's the early and late Wittgenstein in one sentence: Philosophy is mostly nonsense, because the words, as used in that way, don't picture facts and thereby go beyond their logical limits; or, on second thought, it's nonsense, because the words are used metaphysically and go beyond the limits of our everyday language-game.

My girlfriend said I had a pompous name for my mutt dog. So I didn't let her play with little Jedediah Birmingham Hathaway-Titsworth.

June is the most august month.

The first cartographers were given wide latitude.

Imagine a woman raising money to get breast augmentation and her shirt says, "Implants or bust!"

I once dated a woman named Chang Su, who assured me that her oriental massage business was legitimate. But when I asked her what her name meant in Chinese, she said "happy ending."

The most underrated invention in medical history is the placebo. It permits all drugs to be tested properly.

Perry Mason was the only defense attorney who could consistently make his DA look like *hamburger.*

My boss was a good-hearted pyromaniac. For every dollar we raised for charity, he promised to match it.

Whenever the Queen leaves England, she's suddenly abroad.

When a marriage hits an iceberg, men feel like a passenger on the Titanic, because it's women and children first.

My therapist said I started out with a superiority complex and gradually developed an inferiority complex. So I wound up dead even.

2

Next time somebody asks me if I believe in God, I want to say, "Do you mean God as a causal inference, an abstract concept, or an anthropomorphic entity?"

The best book for the student of philosophy to begin with is Bertrand Russell's *Autobiography*. It shows philosophy as a human activity, with a face, and presents the back-story to G.E. Moore and Ludwig Wittgenstein. Russell, Moore, and Wittgenstein were the most prominent and influential philosophers during the first half of the Twentieth Century. The book is also a gateway to other good writers, such as J.M. Keynes and Lytton Strachey.

Nietzsche
He dared to say that morals are a means to an end

And for their survival they must fend.
But this has been swept under the bed
By those who only quote, "God is dead."

If Lizzie Borden had lived in Harlem, she would have said, "Mom, can I axe you a question?"

The son-in-law of Elvis Presley, Michael Jackson, evidently didn't learn from Elvis's death. He became a reclusive drug addict too. They both proved, along with Marilyn Monroe, that talent, looks, money, and celebrity aren't enough. Avoiding self-destructive behaviors is the key.

OK, we tried it Michael Jackson's way. Time for plan B. If you want to make the world a better place, take a look at *someone else* and make a change.

Guys call confident guys "jerks" and complain that girls only date jerks, and women call attractive girls "sluts" and complain that men only date sluts. No wonder people think so many sluts and jerks exist!

Those who didn't invest in the Luxor Hotel and Casino suspected a pyramid scheme.

Egypt should call their national crew team *Cai-Row*.

Imagine if Pete Townsend were not in *Who's Who*.

OJ should have been forced to take a bath with Andrea Yates.

If a girl ever tells you she's a "whistleblower," just tell her you're a whistle.

An abstract for a movie: One teenage girl's struggle with bulimia set against the backdrop of the Oklahoma dustbowl famine.

Philosophy is often called useless. But think of how many people are misled by false notions that philosophy is best suited to debunk.

Deconstruction is just a pretentious excuse for academics to interpret texts any way they please.

Today's shareholders have been reduced to phony capitalists – a million would-be *Scrooges* whom the Board of Directors play for *stooges*.

Unlike men, middle-aged women don't read Plato's works straight through. There's usually a *pause* after the *Meno*.

Gay men must be big fans of baseball. They're always talking about who's going to be the pitcher.

When I finally got over my persecution complex, everyone turned against me.

Funny how spicy girls seem to curry more favor with guys.

I was raised to believe fruits were genderless. So imagine my surprise when I first heard about melon balls. Now people want to ban *trans fats*, which seems homophobic.

A stripper went to the doctor and complained of chest pains. He examined her fully and said, "I think you have acute angina." She said, "Thanks, Doc, but how's my heart?"

Ask a girl if she believes in tit-for-tat. If she does, pat her on the shoulder and say, "OK, there's a *tat*."

I believe in fighting terrorists. If al-Qaeda ever blew three legs off my kitchen table, I'd say, "This will not stand!"

The lion's share of metaphors are too vague. Especially that one.

Facts don't have to conform to theories, but theories have to conform to facts. Remember what tests what.

Days are like golf shots. Each one should set up the next.

Everything has pro's and con's. Water nourishes and drowns. Pretending political policies have no downside is fantasy thinking.

Happiness is the feeling of satisfaction you get from doing what you think you should do and doing it well.

People say that someone can't see the forest for the trees. In philosophy, we should say that they can't see the facts for the words.

3

In relationships, we tend to push others away and then act surprised when they stay away.

Some let alcohol substitute for pride of accomplishment.

Somebody once called me a *snob*, and I responded, "Hey, Mr. Nobody, who the hell do you think you're talking to?" Maybe he had a point...

Love of the past saps affection for the present and future.

The best feeling is doing better than you thought possible.

People say, "Love is the answer," but forget the question was merely, "What's a four-letter word for strong affection?"

The best book for a student of investing to begin with is *Baruch: My Own Story* by Bernard Baruch. He was the son of a Confederate surgeon at Gettysburg and by age thirty-two, in 1902, he had over three million dollars saved up – an astronomical sum for a young man to have earned on Wall Street back then. The book is a history lesson, a life lesson, and an investment guide. The story of his mother's clash with Union troops during the Civil War is worth the price alone.

She spent $6,000 on liposuction and a boob job, when all she needed was to smile.

Sometimes, I imagine that I'm already back from the dead now, with a second chance.

The bad philosopher writes with the license of a poet, not realizing that it is suspended while writing prose.

How come there's no special seating area for psychics at the Kentucky Derby?

Before falling asleep each night, celebrate victories and isolate errors.

All conduct has an opportunity cost. So denigrating even the best course of action is always possible.

To win the war on terror, we must think outside the mosque.

Happiness is satisfying your immediate needs and feeling slightly virtuous about it.

Doing something quickly is a common excuse for doing it poorly.

Replace dogma with means-end analysis.

A litany of adjectives is the sign of someone with no facts.

For each person, there's an ordinary situation in which he will react badly. Often, he's unaware of it and may come to ruin by surprise.

Many academics write not to help the reader understand something but to appear erudite.

Strip joints: a place where men look for *succor* and dancers find one.

If a woman yells at me, I'm not afraid to use the C-word. I say, "Control yourself, please!"

In California, I heard three women were killed by a mudslide. Imagine the size of that glass!

The other day, someone called me immature. I said, "I know you are, but what am I?"

Who you are at fifty is who you were at sixteen writ large.

The doctor said his decision to perform the lobotomy was a no-brainer.

When your argument is *pregnant* with false assumptions, your conclusion is *stillborn*. It's a *miscarriage* of logic.

If politics is the defense of the indefensible, as George Orwell says, then practicing criminal defense law is the art of making the least likely explanation of the evidence seem most likely.

Your currency in a relationship is your approval. If it's honest, it's backed by gold and printable at no cost. But some refuse to issue any. And some issue only a fiat currency.

There are *three* kinds of people in the world. Those who use facile *dichotomies* and a couple of others.

4

If ethics were science, then Socrates would be Galileo.

Today is only yesterday's tomorrow. So we already live in the future.

Each day we trade a spoonful of youth for a spoonful of experience and try to make it a fair trade.

Ambitious people seem immune to shame. It doesn't serve their ends.

Sports prove that you can't play well scared. So don't live scared.

Imagine if dictionaries were moralizing – after the definition of "inspiration," it said, "See perspiration."

The happy man is the wise man, for he knows how to satisfy his desires.

Tourists differ. One is drawn to Londonderry air. Another, to London *derriere*.

We have to remind ourselves that words are just man-made signs. They only have the meaning our collective usage has given them. (Wittgenstein's lesson.) Cheese melted on toast is called "Welsh rabbit." Who the hell started that one?

Education has some benefits. I used to say I'm lazy. Now, I say I'm indolent.

Most wealthy people in Seattle have umbrella insurance.

On the phone, my doctor said that he's a "bored, certified physician." So I responded, "Well, it's never too late for a career change."

They say he's a "*wunderkind*." But is he *kind*, I *wonder?*

You can't take a step forward if you keep kicking yourself.

There is a *best* way of saying anything. This fact keeps writers forever humble. Or humble forever. No, I think it was better the first time.

The saying "Hindsight is 20/20" is wrong. Often, we don't know where the shoe pinches.

Before doing something important, ask what you really *want* to do and then what you honestly imagine the smartest person in the world would do in your spot. Interesting to compare the answers.

The times are changin'. We've gone from a moral condemnation to amoral condom nation.

When they pass on the street, men and women feel unfairly judged by each other. Men pay for the sins of their brothers, and women pay for the sins of their sisters.

Pundits on TV increasingly call things a "mess" – the situation in Iraq, the banking system, the economy. The word spares them the task of learning the specific facts and of describing them exactly. The word is un-illuminating and a sign of someone who hasn't done any homework.

The wordy writer disrespects the reader's time.

To be an adult means to outgrow what you wish the world would be and what you were told it was. Rather, you find out what it is and act accordingly.

Word count is emphasis. Most books and essays falter quietly from undue emphasis. The author rambles on about an unimportant matter and skirts an important one.

It's not what you have done but what you are doing that counts. And others only care about what you can do tomorrow.

Metaphors are similes, which is a metaphor. And similes are like metaphors, which is a simile.

Part of the past is always present.

Fools struggle to improve their weaknesses, while the wise live in their strength.

Science can tell you how to make a gun but not when to use it.

If Orwell is right, and good writing is a "window pane," then bad writing is stained glass. The author tries to impress us but blurs our vision instead.

<u>On growing up</u>

When the parental shriek for your guilt
and shame
Is no longer met with bowed head and self-
blame
But with furrowed brow and cold sneer,
You'll be free of its tyranny, my dear.

5

A philosopher's facile verbal categories blind us to the vast spectrum of nature and psychology.

With their abstractions and reifications, poets give us a false picture of the world.

Your final grade in life is your cumulative happiness, since it measures how clever you have been at knowing and satisfying your particular desires.

Pedantic professors seem to just split hairs not worth splitting – but not infinitives.

Someone once called me a manic-depressive. First, I laughed; then, I cried.

Disorganized people are list-less.

When I said I wanted to be a chiropractor, I was just posturing.

Someone told me he wanted to be a funeral director. I said that's quite an *undertaking*.

And teaching logic is quite a *proposition!*

I imagine that women think golfers make the worst lovers, because golfers have been conditioned to think that the fewest number of strokes wins.

I used to travel. Now I just visit Yahoo! Maps.

How can obesity be a problem when diet books have been bestsellers for the past forty years?

Is there a memory trick for learning how to spell *mnemonic?*

The USA will always be more productive than Europe. They have the metric system. They don't know what it means to go that extra mile.

At college, I minored in nonchalance.

The formula for a bad date: a good-looking guy and a pretty girl both wait to be seduced by the other. Disillusionment.

News headline in the year 2525: *Psychologists discover that the Women's Lib members who chanted "Male chauvinist pigs" were actually female chauvinist pigs.*

On the cruelty of chess. To learn it, you must enjoy it. To enjoy it, you must win. And to win, you must study it so thoroughly that it becomes un-enjoyable.

The rich and poor are more like each other than like the middle-class. The rich get a handout from their family, and the poor get one from their government.

Eat, drink, and be merry. But the last one doesn't follow from the first two.

The best side of vinyl from the 1970's is side one of Elton John's "Captain Fantastic and the Brown Dirt Cowboy."

People take a subconscious stance towards others. Some are leery or adversarial by nature without realizing it. So when they get treated poorly, they are unaware of their role in it.

Displays of wealth usually backfire. The poor think about robbing you, and the rich think you're a show-off.

Those who tell you to ignore slights and injustices are just repeating clichés. Look at your experiences. The avenged injustice stops irking, while the un-avenged one still rankles.

Just like every punch and kick, every slight and insult can be parried and countered.

The energy of frustration is fuel for corrective measures.

If love is a loser's game, then you win by not playing it.

Why do so many rich kids seem like underachievers? Because (i) most people are underachievers, but we notice it more when they are rich; (ii) rich kids can feel important while doing nothing and thereby have less incentive to take risks; (iii) they can afford booze, pot, and other drugs more easily; and (iv) they have more idle time. The Roman poet Horace said, "poverty gave me sufficient boldness to start writing poems." Same with Eminem.

A bachelor may justify staying single with the simple mathematics of expected values and a 50% probability of divorce. On a happiness scale of -100 to +100, he may reason that half of -80 is more bad than half of +60 is good. Risk aversion.

The most common metaphor for our investments, the nest egg, supplies us with an unhelpful image. Better to picture investments as plants in our garden. It reminds us to remove the losers quickly and to let the winners grow tall, thereby forestalling the two chief mistakes investors make: holding losers too long and selling winners too soon. Think of our garden as a showpiece. The nest egg idea brings no similar advantage. In fact, one big egg even suggests a lack of diversification, a disadvantage.

6

Laissez-faire was a capital idea.

My friend once accused me of adopting a phony British accent, like Madonna. So I told him not to call me for a *fortnight*.

Guys think hookers are rich. But many live hand-to-mouth.

Today's honest observer is a step ahead of ancient texts. But teachers lionize the writers of old. Why? Job security – that's what they know.

Show me someone who uses only logic, and I'll show you a doctrinaire fool who wins no real-life arguments. He doesn't get what he wants.

Learning when not to use a gun is more important than learning expert marksmanship.

The saying that conscience makes cowards of us all is wrong, but with alliteration. Conscience can inspire courage. Self-doubt and fear make cowards.

An idea for a project in ethics. Interview people who have violated most or all of the Ten Commandments. Then interview those who have violated none or the fewest. Compare their life stories and levels of happiness. Find the oldest people you can.

The profile of an unhappy person: someone upset daily with some aspect of the world that he cannot change. Accepting the world and how people are is the starting point, which some never arrive at.

An effective response to a question intended to discredit.
TV show guest: I served in the military. Are you a veteran, Glenn?
Glenn Beck: Why do you ask? [With a smile.] Does that mean that as a US citizen, I have no right to comment on my country's military policy, if I am not a veteran?

Why can't you convince some people that astrology is pseudo-psychology? Because they know at least one Taurus who is stubborn, at least one Libra who is... But with over six and a half billion people on the planet now, more than the entire population of the USA is Taurus! And most people are stubborn.

How many people on anti-depressants were previously un-assertive, un-ambitious, or un-skilled? Treating the resulting depression with a pill does not eradicate the cause. If anything, the pill dims the conscience and thereby encrusts the condition.

The most annoying traits of talk-radio hosts: (i) not finishing sentences; (ii) restating the same idea in different words; (iii) saying "you know" and "ah" too much; (iv) using an affected tone-of-voice that indicates a high level of self-satisfaction; and (v) making every story about them.

An overlooked factor in ethics is time spent. One may rank the things he does by importance, but how much time is spent on each? Somebody says he prefers reading to watching TV but spends far more time watching TV, which *reveals* the opposite preference. On the unreliability of *surveys*.

The student-athlete ideal is worth keeping after college. The challenge is becoming our own professor and coach.

Metaphysics has no one landscape to discover, only many to draw. But the drawers act like discoverers.

The most annoying ad on TV: "So where will you be when your diarrhea comes back?" Imagine the president of that advertising company – "That's a winner, Johnson! Let's run with it!"

How can existence pass into nothingness? That's a great example of a bad question in philosophy. The abstract reifications create a false picture. Something as simple as killing a fly seems impossible.

On putting the problem wrong. Before Y2K hit, journalists drummed up fear by saying, "Computers won't know what time it is." Computers never *knew*. Y2K was not a problem of knowledge but of math like any other computer problem.

Very annoying people: those who use activism for self-advancement and call more attention to themselves than to their cause. The Barbi Twins.

Some people will complain no matter what. Even in heaven. "This harp music is driving me nuts!"

Students who learn by rote know the *symbols* but not the facts behind them. Given *Principia Mathematica*, if Bertrand Russell ever played a musical instrument, it should have been the cymbals.

Notice how literally empty some common expressions are: "Enough is enough"; "I'm not myself today"; "It was just one of those things." Yet we rely on them to convey specific ideas. And they do! On the power of idioms.

Under capitalism, the customer is king. Under communism, the customer is powerless. Would you rather be powerless or king? But Marxists focus only on the employer-employee relation, it seems.

The prideful author was upset after his appendix was removed.

Unlike other professors of philosophy, Wittgenstein read no Aristotle. He said he didn't want it to confuse his thinking. How many authors have confused our thinking without our realizing it?

How do you set someone up to fail? By lionizing them and expecting perfection.

Bobby Fischer misspent his prize money on a corrupt church, lost his possessions in storage by not paying the fees, and was punished extra for starting trouble with his jail guards in Japan. He blundered continuously off the chessboard. Checkmated by life.

Learning is frustrating. Thus, some prefer to stop.

Fretting over politics and world events beyond our control is a common trap. Step back and resolve to be entertained by it and to prosper no matter what. George Carlin's detachment was psychological self-defense. (See introductory quotations.)

7

Resilience is asking how you can make this mistake or misfortune work for you in the future. A loss has to be directly offset by a lesson learned to make it palatable.

Legendary coach John Wooden defined success as reaching our unique potential. Trouble is, we never know what it is. So we guess. And we probably guess wrong a lot, demanding too much or too little.

Machiavelli wrote not of the traits that should work for a leader but of those that in fact have worked. He was not an ethicist but an early social scientist. Yet glib moralizers dismiss him as merely unethical.

All agree that the rich should pay their "fair share" of federal income taxes. If 10% of the population paid 10% of the revenues collected, would that be fair? Now the top 10% pay almost 70%, but some claim that *fairness* requires that they pay even more.

If you're constantly surprised by what others do, then you probably don't understand human nature very well. Prediction is the mark of understanding.

Montaigne mistitled his essay, "To philosophize is to learn to die." Rather, it's to learn to live, ephemerally.

"Deliver us from evil." That's a bad way of putting it. Evil is not a place or a thing. So that's a false picture. Better to ask for the wisdom and courage to make good decisions.

Vincent Bugliosi's questioning why God gets credit for good events and escapes blame for bad events is answerable. If something is good, it gets put in the category of God's work. If it's bad, it's put in the category of the Devil's work. God is never tested. He functions rather as a placeholder, the concept of goodness personified.

Some blacks who claim to hate stereotypes and racial profiling seem to think nothing of stereotyping all whites as racists.

If you enjoy solitude, embrace it, and enjoy its benefits, as Isaac Newton did. Many can't, achieve less as a result, and wind up tolerating annoying people too much.

Some useful heuristics:
* **What is the cost-benefit?**
* **Compared to what?**
* **Which is the end and which is the means?**
* **Do we have cause and effect reversed?**
* **Work backwards from the end.**
* **Can this problem be quantified?**
* **Draw a picture of the problem.**
* **Is there a formula or flow chart for this?**
* **Is the problem with the people or with the incentive structure?**

A daunting task is just a series of doable tasks.

The news of the day is 99% irrelevant to our daily life. Yet many act as if it's 90% relevant.

"The sky is falling." A false picture of nature embedded in an everyday expression.

Idea for a modern film *noir*. A man has a daughter, calls her his little "Princess," sends her to a women's college, and pays $200,000 in tuition for her to major in Women's Studies.

After graduation, she comes home, announces she's lesbian, and declares that all men are evil oppressors. Years later, a therapist convinces her that despite her saying that she was never abused, she could have repressed memories of it. The daughter then accuses her father of sexual abuse, ruining his reputation, despite his innocence, just as he pays off the last of her student loans.

A bum on the street once told me: "If someone else is happy, it's his own fault." He held no grudge.

An artist's pride and self-regard can easily get ahead of his ability. Much harder for that to happen to a tennis player or a chess player. Competition keeps you humble.

The smug scholar is wrong to say that knowing the etymology of a word is necessary to understand its "real meaning." Many words have no known etymology, yet their meaning is just as knowable, e.g., *snob, fake, jerk*. Usage is the determinant. Etymology can even mislead. The root of our twelfth month is "ten."

Life is like interval training. Stress, then recovery.

When meeting someone smarter than them, many try to show off how much they know, even when it isn't much, and waste a good opportunity to learn.

On rationalization. After stabbing a beautiful, young pregnant actress to death, Susan Atkins said that she had to have a lot of *love* in her heart to kill a capitalist pig like Sharon Tate.

Some women spend their lives bitterly competing against men and then act surprised that they're still single.

Environmentalism is anti-capitalism with a halo.

The lesson taught by our relatives, friends, and even sit-com stars is that people don't change. Yet we still believe it when they promise to. Why?

Drugs are initially taken with the belief that they *add* something and ended with the realization that they *subtract.*

When you abandon the idea of food as fuel, you are more prone to eat poorly. And when you abandon the idea of sex as procreation, you are more prone to fetish and deviance.

What we say and do to others often surprises even us. And if we resent someone, it will surface sometime, somehow, despite efforts to conceal it.

Anyone who promises to show you the "path to enlightenment" trucks in an empty metaphor, hoping you won't notice.

Those who advocate the danger of man-made global warming must prove their case. In science, as in law, he who asserts must prove. The man-made part ("Man") is simply equal to the current warming ("Warming") minus the amount due to the sun and natural cycles ("Nature"), which has occurred without man's help for millions of years. Thus, the equation is, *Warming - Nature = Man.* But Al Gore cannot know the value of *Man*, as he pretends to, because he does not know the value of *Nature*. He merely guesses that *Nature* is close to zero. This is the flaw in his logic that reporters ignore – as if they refuse to think it through. He puts garbage into computer models and gets garbage out (GI/GO) and plays on our fears to advance his image and agenda. A dangerous vanity.

The words we have for emotional conditions are misty, hard to test, and, as a result, easily misapplied. *Depression* and *loneliness* could be misdiagnosed, for example, and no one would notice.

8

A question every writer should ask: If I read this ten years from now, will I be satisfied?

You can be anything you want to be – many kids are told that line. More honest to tell them, "People usually have few talents, and discovering them may take years, and years more to develop them fully." Mark David Chapman's mother told him he could be anything he wanted, but he discovered he was only mediocre at things. Then he grew to think his former idol, John Lennon, was a hypocrite, so he shot him.

Those who disparage evolution as only a "theory" truck in a misleading sense of the term. Why not jump off a tall building, if the only thing preventing you from flying is a *guess* – the theory of gravitation? Evolution is a theory in the strong sense of that which makes sense of concrete facts, such as fossils, species, genetics, heredity, mutations, sedimentary layers, carbon decay, and so on.

People think attitude is an intangible, but it reduces to tangible facts concerning facial expression, tone of voice, thought pattern, and behavior. Thus, ways to alter attitude.

Very annoying people: those who try to impress you with big words while misusing them in the process.

Florida 2000
If Al Gore's chads got stronger pushes,
We might have all stayed out the Bushes.

If Geraldine Page married Ike Turner, she could have been Geraldine Page-Turner. A good name for an author.

A cruel injustice of love – when fawning over another renders you unlovable in return.

Imagine saying you'd die for the sins of other people and even for those not yet born. Not only is it grandiose, it's illogical. A moral impossibility.

Trying to get basic information from a long magazine article becomes frustrating when the author keeps calling attention to himself by playing a version of the psychological game "Look, Ma, I can dance" rather than sticking to the point.

An algorithm is the final heuristic.

"Soul" is defined as "the disembodied spirit of a dead human." But "spirit" is defined as, "the soul, considered as departing from the body of a person at death."

Legendary investor Bernard Baruch said investors suffered from information overload during the 1950's. Imagine what he'd say now after spending a week watching CNBC, listening to Bloomberg radio, and surfing the Internet.

J.M. Keynes brought some wit to economics, once writing that he didn't want to blame one country in particular for starting WWI, since that was not "germane" to his concern.

Much academic writing is the art of saying something in an impressive manner ambiguously enough so that it can never be refuted. The future reputation of the author is of paramount concern, not whether the reader actually learns anything.

Jim Brown proved that minding your own business is not enough. He never started trouble, but when it found him, he overreacted and got too physical. Righteous anger is dangerous, for it makes you feel justified. As Aristotle said, *proportionality* is as difficult as it is important.

If somebody hits you, and you don't want to hit him back nor let him get away with it, arrest him for battery on the spot, forcefully, and ask someone to call the police. A good way to get justice without flattening someone.

Much of philosophy, especially of the "S is P" variety, is the splitting of hairs that don't need splitting and playing with inaccurate models of our actual language.

"My heart and soul are in this city," said a coach on TV. What hard facts does that misleading image actually reduce to? It permits some general predictions about his future conduct. That's all.

Sitting in an armchair and imagining how the facts *must be* is a bad way to learn them. Descartes wrote, "It is contrary to reason to say that there is a vacuum or space in which there is absolutely nothing."

A teenaged girl on TV...
Jenny Jones: You have sex for money, don't you?
Girl: Yes.
Jenny Jones: Then you're a prostitute?
Girl: No, I'm not!
(On how words are often admitted or denied in real life based on whether they connote approval or disapproval, regardless of their accuracy.)

Is a given law *just* or a given action *moral?* Maybe, but that needs some demonstration beyond mere citation to a book.

Wittgenstein once wrote, "Why do we feel a grammatical joke to be *deep*?" For instance, when John Lennon sang, "But listen to the color of your dreams," it was not profundity but nonsense.

William James divided philosophers into two camps: the tough-minded and the tender-minded. I'd divide them into those who favor *prescription* and those who favor *description.*

Richard Feynman reminded us not to mistake the man-made symbol for the thing itself and to avoid rote learning, because it's fragile. See past the equation to nature.

When someone says he forgets what a P/E ratio is, I suspect he never really knew. Once you see the facts behind the symbols, you can't forget. Just picture a company's net profit and divide it by the number of shares outstanding to get E. Then divide the current price of one share by E to get the ratio. Or just think of it as the *earnings multiple* – the number you must multiply E by to get today's share price, P.

Ecclesiastes was wrong. Under the sun, something new happens every day. No two days are alike. Each has its own interesting surprises to wake up for. A matter of being a *leveler* or a *sharpener* of distinctions – two other camps in philosophy.

Grandpa was a fortune-teller. He had a glass eye and a crystal ball.

Many seem so used to aiming low that they forget that aiming high is the best way to go farther than they otherwise would, even if they fall short of their target.

Cause and effect are not neat and discrete in real life. Is a woman bitter because she does not have a man, or does she not have a man because she's bitter? Effects become causes and so on.

9

Some Russian farmers once grew vegetables poorly. An agronomist told them their soil was sandy, better for grapes. They planted a vineyard and grew rich. People are like soil.

The pseudo-intelligentsia see the facts dimly, if at all, and rely on showy metaphors instead.

Investment pundits mix metaphors to an annoying degree, saying things like, "When stocks hit nose-bleed levels, consumers threw in the towel. So now the Fed is trying to electroshock a comatose economy back to life." No one objects, though.

I saw an article on the alleged "smartest" man in the world. He read every volume of the *Encyclopedia Britannica* in a year or so. He may have acquired plenty of information, but did he get any *smarter*? Probably not. And how much does he remember? He had a flawed passive model of learning. Compare merely reading the rules of chess vs. becoming a strong player.

The newspaper said that each Marine is sent into battle with a rifle and three magazines. That's no time to read!

When hundreds of Swift Boat veterans criticized John Kerry, major network news stations deemed the criticism not credible, despite the veterans having served alongside him. Then when somebody from the Texas National Guard criticized George Bush, Dan Rather deemed that credible and presented documents that proved forged. Rather tried to save face afterwards by saying the documents were "forged but accurate" and denied any bias. But the bias resides in letting politics determine who is deemed credible.

If someone came here from another planet and saw businessmen get up early and go to work, while others went to a welfare office, got tax money, bought booze, and watched TV – he'd think the poor enslave the rich.

Idea for a movie. One day a child is born not as a musical or sports prodigy but as a prodigy in charm. He's great at making friends, selling, negotiating, persuading – so much so that politicians, law firms, and even SWAT teams hire him, although he's only thirteen.

Efficacy first, then efficiency.

Rush Limbaugh repeats the saying, "Brevity is the soul of wit," without thinking. The soul of wit is surprise and cogency.

Like Feynman, Wittgenstein is a hero to those who prize intellectual honesty. He was always disdainful of pretense and nonsense and curious about finding the limits of language. But its limits are invisible and easily transgressed, creating misunderstandings and nonsense that often go undetected.

If you are angry and unsure why, someone has probably threatened your status in some subtle way.

No sense fighting your natural likes, dislikes, and temperament. Recall Dave Chappelle's freaking out and walking away from his successful TV show and later saying you have to accept yourself eventually "for better or worse."

While reading Sylvia Plath's diary, I was most struck by how she berated herself for not learning shorthand, not writing more stories, and not making better use of her time – all while getting the best grades in her college class. She was her own worst critic. And she wound up killing herself. A lesson there in how *not* to talk to yourself. Compare others who give themselves pep talks.

A bad philosopher will give you a universal for three particulars.

Some people think they are not communicating when they keep their mouth shut, not realizing that they are saying a lot already with their eyes, face, posture, and even clothing.

Jesus said the kingdom of God is *within*, because the voice of conscience is the voice of God. Thus, it's available to agnostics and atheists as well.

When I was a freshman in college, I asked an old professor of English who he thought the best writer was, and he said Carl Becker, a professor of history at Cornell in the 1930's. Not Hemingway, not Shakespeare. I had never heard of Becker but have since read his letters and his book *The Declaration of Independence.* The little-known Becker, a master of the subordinate clause, ranks in the upper tier, along with Orwell, E.B. White, and J.L. Austin – all have a fluid, graceful, transparent style.

Parts of San Francisco are so politically correct that even lactose *intolerance* is frowned upon.

Why do people overestimate their intelligence, judgment, and moral goodness? Because it feels good. Consider the opposite.

The person on the street may wonder why the Supreme Court has so many split decisions (5-4, 6-3, 7-2), if the law is the law. Laws and principles intersect the facts in manifold ways. Judges on courts of final appeal sometimes face the dilemma of following a prominent rule to a result they consider unjust or finding some principled exception to it. Strict constructionists, who are devotees of the Plain-meaning rule, tend to follow a statute regardless of consequence and are chary to deviate from case precedent, as exemplified by the dissent in *MacPherson v. Buick Motor Co.,* or to legislate from the bench, as shown in *Roberson v. Rochester Folding Box Co.* While judicial activists, who are devotees of sociological jurisprudence, tend to feel less hamstrung by statutes and cases and are more apt to tap dance their way to a result they deem just, as in *Marvin v. Marvin* and *Dillon v. Legg*.

Baseball fans are stuck in a verbal muddle when they debate, "Good pitching beats good hitting." One could say that the good pitching mentioned is not really facing good hitting at the time and insist on the reverse. Compare the question in philosophy: What happens when an irresistible force meets an immovable object? It looks like a question about facts, but it's really about *words*. On the importance of the philosophy of language.

Roughnecks who put down philosophy nonetheless get stuck in verbal muddles of their own making. When E.B. White worked on a cruise ship after college, he noticed the engine crew would endlessly debate the question, "Who makes the ship go?" Evidently, none thought to reject the question as ambiguous.

A key to Jimmy Buffett's likability is his humility: "Some people claim that there's a woman to blame, but I know, it's my own damn fault." Women appreciate that sentiment, and men respect it too.

For fun, no matter what shirt a guy's wearing, tell him, "Now they sell a version of that shirt for men too, you know."

Remember that you only have to transpose two letters to go from "tired" to "tried."

On the danger of pronouns...
John: Nick's father died.
Mary: Oh, is he OK?
John: No, he's dead.

If some spoiled kid tells you it's easy to be the best at something, because his parents told him so, tell him to enter a golf, chess, or martial arts tournament and see. Competition teaches humility and respect for others.

Once you stop trusting your own inner voice, you're lost. Even if it's been wrong before, it's still the best guide you've got.

Do all herbalists give sage advice?

10

The problem with a generous social safety-net? —Able-bodied workers use it as a hammock.

Einstein said he usually didn't think in words but in images. Yet we focus so much on learning and teaching verbal rather visual thinking.

In parts of Wisconsin, cheese has become a cottage industry.

Some people can keep their sense of humor no matter what, like that guy who fell into a wood chipper. His last words were, "Open casket."

The most elusive metaphor is the one for life itself – a poor player that struts and frets; dust in the wind; a soul's proving ground to see if it deserves eternal reward or suffering; a brief candle; a bowl of cherries...

Halle Berry suggested that racial *animus* prevented a black woman from winning an Oscar for best actress until she did it. Let's see her back up that charge, year-by-year, and tell us which black actresses were better than the winners. And then look at every year that Al Pacino didn't win in the 1970's and 80's. With Ms. Berry's logic, that's proof of bias against Italian-Americans too. Besides, Jackie Mason raised the most credible claim of racism in Hollywood, when he asked, "Where are all the Chinese tap dancers?" Maybe Susan Estrich should investigate that glass ceiling.

Our mind has a mind of its own. Mistakes will be gone over until they are understood. Threats will be assessed and prepared for, for our own good, whether we like it or not.

A hackneyed formula I can do without: "X is *no stranger* to Y." Just say what dealings X has had with Y and quit stalling.

Hubris tarnishes your quality of life, because it leads you to expect greater results than you are capable of at a given point in time. So you chastise yourself or quit, not realizing the root of the problem. Picture someone on vacation, in the lap of luxury, miserable over his golf game. Haughty expectations.

The dominant device in Seinfeld's comedy? Rhetorical questions. They get us thinking along.

A good item to send into space so aliens learn about our culture is a tub of "I can't believe it's not butter!" Picture those little green men trying to figure out what type of civilization would name a product that. Their top scientist finally says, "I'd love to know what this 'butter' is – but all we know for sure is that this ain't it!"

The expression "Once bitten, twice shy" low-balled it. Some are shy forever after.

Politicians who continuously mention the "injustices of capitalism" should be called on it. There's a simple justice in voluntary exchange.

Why do productive people, such as G.E. Moore, consider themselves lazy? Perhaps, because they remember one day in particular when they accomplished a lot and think they could repeat it everyday, if only they tried harder. But peak performance is rare, by definition.

I think grief counselors are a sign of a whiny-ass nanny state gone wrong. If anything, I imagine they keep wounds open longer and make kids feel worse by encouraging victim status and self-pity. And if some kids show strength, I bet it's treated as false bravado and discouraged.

Is nicotine a drug or a poison? It depends on the dosage. Same with love.

When you get older, it's discouraging to see words in a little pocket dictionary that you don't already know, e.g., *dybbuk, wimple... horology*, which isn't what you pimps think.

You can't learn something until you admit you don't know it, and pride keeps you from admitting it. Thus, pride keeps you ignorant.

The person with the burden of proof has a disadvantage. Notice how Bill O'Reilly often shifts the burden of proof to his TV show guests. He'll state his thesis and rather than support it, he'll say, "How am I wrong?" And if his guest can't refute him, Bill acts as if he's been vindicated. But his guest could say, "No, the real question is, how are you right, Bill? Can you support that thesis?"

Ever notice that when you eat a French vanilla ice cream cone, you tend to use your tongue more?

I'm tired of investment pundits saying gold has "intrinsic value." Try eating it. Food, water, shelter, clothing, and medicine have intrinsic value. People value gold based on its utility as a metal, on its history, and on current sentiment, which is fickle. From 1980-2000, gold fell from roughly $800/0z to roughly $300/0z. But the opportunity cost was greater than the $500 lost. With interest compounded at 5% per year, $800 in cash grew to $2,100, a *seven-fold* gain over that gold coin which only fell in price and earned no interest. Granted, gold was worth $38 per oz. in 1972 and $988 at one point in 2008, for a twenty-six-fold gain, while the same amount of cash in 1972, at 5% interest compounded over that time, would have only gone up about six-fold. So, like any investment, the buy-in price remains key. Yet, apart from supply & demand, gold has no *intrinsic* value.

The first step toward happiness is eliminating sources of unhappiness. Then try asking what you can do this week that will make you proud next week.

I worked in a law office with two secretaries. The boss gave a different impression of his leadership style with each. The heavy, middle-aged lady took his gruff orders. The pretty young one didn't, so he politely asked her for things. They both got what they tolerated. Business authors talk about a boss's style as if it's a constant, but it's often a variable.

I give all good actors their props.

Good music climbs a mountain in your mind.

Rush Limbaugh said that when he began in radio, he was given advice at the station on how to broadcast. Following it made him worse. Then he started to model those who were good broadcasters and improved. On learning by rule vs. example.

Over the centuries, I wonder how many nuns secretly wanted to be like Mary and hoped for a virgin birth. An odd conception.

How many of us are simply too scared to do something but don't realize it, because we have convinced ourselves that we're too prudent, cautious, or smart to attempt it?

What was the sport that most influenced Bruce Lee's style of martial arts? *–Fencing.*

When someone criticizes a minority on a matter of fact, he is sometimes called a racist in return. Thus, his motives are merely guessed at, despite other facts being at issue. The one called a racist should shift the burden of proof to his accuser, demanding he substantiate the charge. And if the charge is baseless, that should discredit the one making it. Possible names for this fallacy: the Guessed-motive fallacy, the Imputed-motive fallacy, or the Ghost-motive fallacy.

11

If you are disrespected and feel the urge to hit somebody, don't forget to give them a chance to apologize first. Some forget this mutually-convenient resolution and fight straightaway.

When both the guy and the girl play hard-to-get, no one's gettin' any!

If you crumble at being called ugly, gay, vain, dumb, racist – or whatever is just made-up on the spot – then you are nearly as troubled as your accuser. The world becomes a more dangerous place when you are so easily defeated. Getting embarrassed is just beating yourself.

To stick with a workout, it must satisfy you on an emotional, animal level, not just intellectually.

I have a new *formula* for identifying stock market bottoms, which present good buying opportunities. Divide the stock market's P/E ratio by its dividend yield. At true bear market lows, it should fall below two. For example, in 1974, the P/E of the S&P 500 was 9.1 and its yield was 4.7%. In 1980, the P/E was 8.1 and the yield was 5.3%. I've never heard this ratio mentioned before and call it the *PED ratio.* In an overvalued market, the ratio can go above twenty, as in the year 2000, when the P/E was 27.1 and the yield was 1.1%. In an historically average market, the P/E is around 16 and the yield is around 4%, for a PED ratio of around four. Think of it as a barometer of stock market value on a scale of roughly 1-20.

Socially, many seem to think that if they don't do anything, they can't do anything wrong. But doing nothing when something is expected of you is a sin too, of omission.

Certain things are best kept private. Too bad we only learn that afterwards.

People say not to dwell in the past, but that's a good way to see your future. Habits form, patterns repeat. In work, sleep, exercise, relations, sex, food.

I prefer honest pride to false modesty, but outright conceit is so off-putting that some don't dare approach it. Joyce Carol Oates said she's never been proud of her books, because pride is a sin. But don't envy that; that's is a sin too.

If you skipped your college graduation or had a boring commencement speaker, adopt a surrogate speech as your own. I did. Mario Cuomo gave a poignant and timeless speech to the graduates of Iona College in 1984, published in William Safire's *Lend Me Your Ears.*

Unfortunately, the sort of "grammar" error Wittgenstein warned against has no technical name in philosophy. I suggest calling it a *Devonshire error,* because Wittgenstein once explained it using that county. He said that a philosopher's toying with a word that has an established meaning is akin to being dissatisfied with a boundary on the map and wishing to redraw it, although no other facts will change.

Those who say, "No one can be *objective,*" as some coffee-shop philosophers do, abuse language unwittingly, for we use that word everyday with perfect sense for people who set aside their subjective inclination to do X in favor of doing Y. Doing Y in that case, such as declining to take an illicit tax deduction, is what we would call an *objective* reading of the tax code. Now if some people want to redefine the word "objective" to describe only some nebulous surreal quality, then they are taking undue liberties with an everyday English word that already has a meaning determined by the history of its use. Many disputes in philosophy involve this sort of error. A Devonshire error.

Regardless of what we tell ourselves or tell others, we intend all the reasonable and probable consequences of our actions.

I wonder if people who claim to have Social Anxiety Disorder (SAD) think social situations are all roses for others. With all the hustlers, intimidators, and snobs out there, a defensive posture is warranted by anyone sensible. SAD seems like a suspect disorder, prone to over-diagnosis. And disorders create patients, who generate *fees.*

Generally, kids aren't taught how to read dictionaries properly and are confused by the many numbered *senses* of a word, wrongly assuming that the first one is the best. The senses are arranged in historical order, with the most recent last, so the first one is the most dated.

Annoying when a pedantic pseudo-scholar insists the etymology and the first numbered sense must always hold sway.

Why read a dictionary? To find the right word for your occasion, which may require rejecting the colloquialism, the slang, the jargon, the genteelism, or the vulgarism. So what's left? What lexicographers call the "invisible" word, the one that expresses your meaning so clearly that it calls no attention to itself.

Thinking in clichés isn't thinking deeply.

The ambitious investor avoids complete diversification, because he wants to move from *beta* to *alpha*.

Wittgenstein's notion of "seeing as" is where the poet and the philosopher meet in the road, though the poet uses verse and metaphor and the philosopher uses prose and simile.

On TV, the sexy and charming Jenny McCarthy interviewed a group of young women in bikinis by a hotel-casino pool. She asked why it was so hard to meet a guy in Las Vegas. One girl said it was because the good-looking ones can be counted on one hand, and the rest are "dorks." The other girls nodded. So looks are their criterion? I thought women called men shallow for that. Worse, the girls have unwittingly adopted a frame of mind that allows them to dismiss 100% of men automatically – 99% are dorks and the rest are stuck-up playboys. So they can now feel good about never meeting any guys, not realizing that they secretly dismiss them all for one reason or the other. In return, guys could do the same, classifying all girls as either dykes, bitches, or ho's.

Funny how those who consider themselves the most *caring* say the way to solve the health care crisis is to have someone else pay for their health care. How might they solve a *lunch crisis*? By asking you to pay for their lunch?

I'd like to coin the term Post-Scholastic Stress Disorder (PSSD), if it hasn't been invented yet. Despite being out of school for over twenty years, I've had recurring nightmares about being late for class, missing tests, or having to write papers under impossible deadlines. Apparently, the subconscious mind thinks that if these things happened once, they can happen again. So my advice to students is don't miss class, tests, or procrastinate on papers, or it may come back to haunt you later while you sleep.

If only the world were not like this or that, I'd...
No, given that it is like this and that, what's
your best move?

Example of a bad question: "Do you believe in
Zion?" Vague and pretentious! Best to respond,
"Which sense of 'Zion'? The old City of David,
Jerusalem today, the land of Israel, the Jewish
people, heaven, or the theocracy of God?"

While floating in space, we can't push anything
away from us, because we lack a foundation.
The same with our lives. We must stand on
some inner rock to push from. It may seem like
picking one arbitrarily, but it feels more like
discovering one that's already there.

It's fun to see investment pundits restate the
clichés of the week – we're still de-leveraging,
welcome to the *new normal*, it's just a counter-
cyclical correction – then balk when asked
what that means we should buy or sell now, as
a result.

A common formula I can do without: telling
us what something is *not*, when it merely rules
out an extreme or impossible case that was
never in doubt. "It's not the end of the world."
"It won't kill ya." They waste time, distract us

with an irrelevancy, and avoid saying what's really going on.

Sometime, ask yourself what you are against and what you are for. I'm against fallacy, poetic nonsense, inapt jargon, inefficiency, fraud, pretentiousness, pedantry, loaded language, pity ploys, sentimental twaddle, group-think, moral posturing, holier-than-thou elitism, and political correctness. I'm for an emperor-has-no-clothes sort of insight, courage, and logic that is Feynmanesque and Wittgensteinian, where fact trumps theory, no matter how entrenched the theory. I'm for elegant simplicity without ornament and a Tiger Woods sort of quiet confidence and competence without delusion, boasting, claptrap, or ballyhoo.

Growing up in America. From inquisitive to acquisitive.

Someone once said that happiness is *brought to* something not gotten from it. Think of a workout or doing the dishes.

12

To the pompous poets
Angelou makes it plain, as does Robert Frost,
But you obscure at a cost.
When the reader has to translate,
The disguise in meaning is too great.
So forget the pretentious and arcane
And try to make it plain.

"Failure" is a misleading noun, because it suggests a concrete thing, as in "Avoid failure" or "He's a failure." This is a false picture of reality. Better to see an activity as having degrees-of-success or to use the verb "fail."

Imagine a serial killer asked why he killed so many, and he says, "I don't know. I guess I'm just a people person."

Seeing someone quote scripture as an authority to someone who doesn't consider it authoritative is like watching someone fire a gun, but a little flag comes out instead of a bullet.

An important word for understanding the meaning of a word was never taught in my school. *Polysemy.* Words are like a jewel, with many bezels shining uniquely from different angles. It's hard for kids to grasp this. "What does it *really* mean?" they will ask. A bogus question based on a false picture of word meaning.

J.L. Austin and Wittgenstein ran along the same rails. Both rejected the idea that words have "essences." Both spotted nonsense questions when others didn't. But I've seen no evidence that Wittgenstein ever read Austin. Austin read Wittgenstein, however – once reaching for a copy of *Philosophical Investigations*, while advising a graduate student, saying, "Let's see what Witters has to say about that." A nice moment in history.

As rich as English is thought to be, with over a quarter million words, it's odd that the Greeks and French have two words for "know," in order to make finer distinctions, but we don't. (French: *savoir, connaitre.* Greek: *techne, episteme.*)

People who irk me:
* **Those who say "i.e." when they mean "e.g."**
* **Those who say "per se" every five minutes.**
* **Those who deliberately use "vis-a'-vis" at a job interview.**
* **Those who say "you know what I'm sayin" at least once in every sentence.**

Whether you are *dirt poor* or *filthy rich*, apparently, you still need to wash up. Strange. And saying a rich guy *took a bath* means he got *cleaned out*. Then people say he's looking for a way to *clean up*. But he must already be clean!

The best essay writers, in both style and content, over the past twenty years have been Thomas Sowell, a conservative, and Susan Estrich, a liberal.

Philosophers have the best toolkit for debunking rhetoric and exposing fallacy and are, therefore, well suited for jury duty.

What do you call someone with a Ph.D. in philosophy? —Waiter!

Merely having the term "end-in-itself" in philosophy does not ensure that it actually has a referent. Supposing that it does was G.E. Moore's mistake.

People who object to no-fault divorce, which began around 1971 in the USA, forget that the British tradition of requiring *grounds* for divorce led to shams. When Bertrand Russell wanted a divorce in 1920 from his first wife, he had to deliberately stage an act of adultery.

Kids working at their first job aren't sure how to talk to the boss. Kids, if you're ever late to work, and your boss says, "You should have been here at 8 AM!" act all excited and say, "Why? What happened at 8 AM?"

A college guy met a pretty, young girl working in the Peace Corps who told him she wanted to be a missionary. He said, "That's quite a *position.*"

An antique dealer makes his future in the past.

An unnecessary stipulative term is a *capital* offense.

I once tried to join a group of anarchists, but they had too many rules.

According to the James-Lange theory, which says emotions are determined by bodily sensations, exercise *should* work wonders.

Why did the pimp get slapped? He was acting too big for his bitches.

A message to all journalists. Your continued reliance on the terms "nightmare" and "wake-up call" is putting me to sleep. "What started out as a dream vacation turned into a nightmare for one Wichita family..." or "This near-miss now serves as a wake-up call." Same hackneyed formula.

Gambling is the road to displeasure. Economists call it the principle of *diminishing marginal utility.* The usefulness of that hundred-dollar bill you are risking is worth more to you than the usefulness of the hundred-dollar bill you hope to win.

People who are tone-deaf tend to avoid playing music, but people who are relationship-deaf seem to keep trying, not sure who is at fault. "Is it me, or is it her?"

I wonder if a pastry chef has ever had a Napoleon complex.

Whoever said to just ignore disrespectful people was wrong. Better to straighten them out quickly before things get worse.

Mother Theresa may have been virtuous, but she looked *hoary*.

Imagine someone trying to downplay the War on Terror by saying that al-Qaeda threats are no news, and no news is good news. So al-Qaeda threats are good news! The fallacy of equivocation.

Granted, the cyclical positions of the moon, planets, and stars create very slight changes in the gravitational forces on earth. But astrologers have shown no logical link to human psychological development, which they must do in order to connect days of birth to personality traits in any credible way.

Talk radio and cable news & comment shows present a daily set of reasons to be outraged at our politicians, political parties, and mainstream journalists. The shows of Mark Levin and Glenn Beck, for example. Yet after repeated indignant rants, viewers are left with anxiety and rage but no real outlet, since we are powerless to stop Medicare fraud, illegal immigration, political self-dealing, welfare fraud, and tax waste. We have only one vote every few years. So these shows produce frustration and create outrage junkies who lose focus on their own problems, where their emotional energy could do more good.

13

Back when more men than women enrolled in college each year, feminists clamored for gender equality in enrollments. But now that more women than men enroll in college each year, feminists are curiously silent, which indicates they never really wanted *equality*.

On Paradox

A dialogue in the style of Plato.

[Socrates walks into his neighbor's house.]

Socrates: Is that your chariot I saw outside?

Encephalitis: Yes, it is, and it is not!

Socrates: Don't talk like a sophist, man! Which is it?

Encephalitis: Well, I took the wheels off for repair, so my entire chariot is not there together. Gotcha!

Socrates: I could see the wheels were off. No need to contradict yourself.

Encephalitis: I thought it was clever and am rather fond of paradox, aren't you?

Socrates: Not for its own sake. The way you say, "it is, and it is not," you merely change the meaning of "it" to avoid an underlying contradiction.

Encephalitis: How so?

Socrates: The first "it" refers to the chariot as a set of parts, and the second "it" refers to it as a fully-assembled unit.

Encephalitis: But philosophy is less fun your way.

Socrates: But your way is mere false profundity. You blend contradiction and equivocation and call it a "paradox." That's misleading.

Encephalitis: OK, whatever. Now let's have some lemonade. Notice the way I make it. It's sweet, and yet it's not sweet!

Socrates: Sure, pour me some. [Looks to audience, smiles, and shakes his head.]

<u>Watching CNBC</u>
An economist was asked, "What do workers now fear?"
And as if to show the cost of education dear,
In fancy words she became quickly mired,
When all she meant was that they might get fired.

If anyone ever asks you if you're *stuck-up*, just act like the President behind a lectern and say, "I'm not taking any more questions at this time."

I'd like to bring a foreigner who is learning English into a supermarket and ask him to point out the foods that we use as euphemisms for money. If he points to cucumbers, coconuts, and cupcakes, I'd say, "No, but that would cost about ten *clams*." If he then points to broccoli, blueberries, and biscuits, I'd say, "No, but that would cost about eight *bananas*." If he asks how to learn English better, I'd say, "Take a full-immersion course, if you have the *lettuce*. But it takes some *bread* to do that."

Printed in the United States
by Baker & Taylor Publisher Services